William James
IS LIFE WORTH LIVING?

William James

Is Life Worth Living?

Spinebill Press

© Spinebill Press 2021

All rights reserved. Apart from any fair dealing for the
purposes of private study, research, criticism or review
permitted under the Australian Copyright Act 1968,
no part may be stored or reproduced by any process
without prior permission. Enquiries should
be made to the publisher.

Spinebill Press
Katoomba NSW, Australia
spinebillpress.com

 A catalogue record for this book is available from the National Library of Australia

ISBN 978 0 6485315 6 2

Design and typography by Michel Streich
Typeset in Caslon

Note to the Reader

The address contained in this book was originally given before the Young Men's Christian Association of Harvard University, in May, 1895. It was afterwards repeated before the Society for Ethical Culture of Philadelphia and the School of Applied Ethics at Plymouth. It was printed in the *International Journal of Ethics* for October, 1895, and, the demand for it having been so great, we are glad to have the permission of the author and of the management of the *Journal* to republish it in more convenient form.

The author desires us to add that he owes his application of the quotation with which the address closes, to Mr. W. M. Salter, who used it in a similar way in an article in the *Index* for August 24, 1882.

PHILADEPHIA, 1896

Is Life Worth Living?

Is Life Worth Living?

When Mr. Mallock's book with this title appeared some fifteen years ago, the jocose answer that "it depends on *the liver*" had great currency in the newspapers. The answer that I propose to give to-night cannot be jocose. In the words of one of Shakespeare's prologues,

I come no more to make you laugh ; things now,
That bear a weighty and a serious brow,
Sad, high, and working, full of state and woe,

must be my theme. In the deepest heart of all of us there is a corner in which the ultimate mystery of things works sadly, and I know not what such an Association as yours intends nor what you ask of those whom you invite to address you, unless it be to lead you from the surface glamour of existence and for an hour at least to make you heedless to the buzzing and jigging and vibration of small interests and excitements that form the tissue of our ordinary consciousness. Without further explanation or apology, then, I ask you to join me in turning an attention, commonly too unwilling, to the profounder bass note of life. Let us search the lonely depths for an hour together and see what answers in the last folds and recesses of things our question may find.

I

With many men the question of life's worth is answered by a temperamental optimism that makes them incapable of believing that anything seriously evil can exist. Our dear old Walt Whitman's works are the standing textbook of this kind of optimism; the mere joy of living is so immense in Walt Whitman's veins that it abolishes the possibility of any other kind of feeling.

To breathe the air, how delicious!
To speak, to walk, to seize something by the hand! ...
To be this incredible God I am! ...
O amazement of things, even the least particle!
spirituality of things! ...
I too carol the Sun, usher'd or at noon, or as now, setting,
I too throb to the brain and beauty of the earth and of
all the growths of the earth. ...

I sing to the last the equalities, modern or old,
I sing the endless finales of things,
I say Nature continues – glory continues,

I praise with electric voice.
For I do not see one imperfection in the universe.
And I do not see one cause or result lamentable at last.

So Rousseau, writing of the nine years he spent at Annecy, with nothing but his happiness to tell:

How tell what was neither said nor done nor even thought, but tasted only and felt, with no object of my felicity but the emotion of felicity itself. I rose with the sun and I was happy; I went to walk and I was happy; I saw 'Maman' and I was happy; I left her and I was happy. I rambled through the woods and over the vine slopes, I wandered in the valleys, I read, I lounged, I worked in the garden, I gathered the fruits, I helped at the indoor work, and happiness followed me everywhere; it was in no one assignable thing; it was all within myself; it could not leave me for a single instant.

If moods like this could be made permanent and constitutions like these universal, there would never be any occasion for such discourses as the present one. No philosopher would seek to prove articulately that life is worth living, for the fact that it absolutely is so would vouch for itself and the problem disappear in the vanishing of the question rather than in the coming of anything like a reply.

But we are not magicians to make the optimistic temperament universal; and alongside of the deliverances of temperamental optimism concerning life, those of temperamental pessimism always exist and oppose to them a standing refutation. In what is called circular insanity, phases of melancholy succeed phases of mania, with no outward cause that we can discover, and often enough to one and the same well person life will offer incarnate radiance today and incarnate dreariness tomorrow, according to the fluctuations of what the older medical books used to call the concoction of the humours. In the words of the newspaper joke, "it depends on the liver." Rousseau's ill-balanced constitution undergoes a change, and behold him in his latter evil days a prey to melancholy and black delusions of suspicion and fear. And some men seem launched upon the world even from their birth with souls as incapable of happiness as Walt Whitman's was of gloom, and they have left us their messages in even more lasting verse than his – the exquisite Leopardi, for example, or our own contemporary, James Thomson, in that pathetic book, *The City of Dreadful Night*, which I think is less well-known than it should be for its literary beauty, simply because men are afraid to quote its words – they are so gloomy and at the same time so sincere. In one place the poet describes a congregation gathered to listen to a preacher in a great unillumined cathedral at night. The sermon is too long to quote, but it ends thus:

O Brothers of sad lives! they are so brief;
A few short years must bring us all relief:
Can we not bear these years of laboring breath?
But if you would not this poor life fulfil,
Lo, you are free to end it when you will,
Without the fear of waking after death. –

The organ-like vibrations of his voice,
Thrilled through the vaulted aisles and died away;
The yearning of the tones which bade rejoice
Was sad and tender as a requiem lay:
Our shadowy congregation rested still
As brooding on that 'End it when you will.'

Our shadowy congregation rested still,
As musing on that message we had heard
And brooding on that 'End it when you will';
Perchance awaiting yet some other word;
When keen as lightning through a muffled sky
Sprang forth a shrill and lamentable cry: –

The man speaks sooth, alas! the man speaks sooth.
We have no personal life beyond the grave;
There is no God; Fate knows nor wrath nor ruth:
Can I find here the comfort which I crave?

In all eternity I had one chance,
One few years' term of gracious human life:
The splendors of the intellect's advance,
The sweetness of the home with babes and wife;

The social pleasures with their genial wit;
The fascination of the worlds of art;
The glories of the worlds of nature lit
By large imagination's glowing heart;

The rapture of mere being, full of health;
The careless childhood and the ardent youth.
The strenuous manhood winning various wealth.
The reverend age serene with life's long truth:

All the sublime prerogatives of Man;
The storied memories of the times of old,
The patient tracking of the world's great plan
Through sequences and changes myriadfold.

This chance was never offered me before;
For me the infinite past is blank and dumb:
This chance recurreth never, nevermore
Blank, blank for me the infinite To-come.

And this sole chance was frustrate from my birth,
A mockery, a delusion; and my breath
Of noble human life upon this earth
So racks me that I sigh for senseless death.

My wine of life is poison mixed with gall,
My noonday passes in a nightmare dream,
I worse than lose the years which are my all:
What can console me for the loss supreme?

Speak not of comfort where no comfort is.
Speak not at all: can words make foul things fair?
Our life's a cheat, our death a black abyss:
Hush, and be mute envisaging despair. –

This vehement voice came from the northern aisle
Rapid and shrill to its abrupt harsh close;
And none gave answer for a certain while,
For words must shrink from these most wordless woes;
At last the pulpit speaker simply said.
With humid eyes and thoughtful, drooping head, –

My Brother, my poor Brothers, it is thus:
This life holds nothing good for us.
But it ends soon and nevermore can be;
And we knew nothing of it ere our birth.
And shall know nothing when consigned to earth;
I ponder these thoughts and they comfort me.

"It ends soon and nevermore can be", "Lo, you are free to end it when you will" – these verses flow truthfully from the melancholy Thomson's pen, and are in truth a consolation for all to whom, as to him, the world is far more like a steady den of fear than a continual fountain of delight. That life is *not* worth living the whole army of suicides declare – an army whose rollcall, like the famous evening drumbeat of the British army, follows the sun round the world and never terminates. We, too, as we sit here in our comfort, must "ponder these things" also, for we are of one substance with these suicides, and their life is the life we share. The plainest intellectual integrity, nay, more, the simplest manliness and honour, forbid us to forget their case.

"If suddenly," says Mr. Ruskin, "in the midst of the enjoyments of the palate and lightnesses of heart of a London dinner party, the walls of the chamber were parted, and through their

gap the nearest human beings who were famishing and in misery were borne into the midst of the company feasting and fancy free – if, pale from death, horrible in destitution, broken by despair, body by body they were laid upon the soft carpet, one beside the chair of every guest, would only the crumbs of the dainties be cast to them – would only a passing glance, a passing thought, be vouchsafed to them? Yet the actual facts, the real relation of each Dives and Lazarus, are not altered by the intervention of the house wall between the table and the sickbed by the few feet of ground (how few!) which are, indeed, all that separate the merriment from the misery."

II

To come immediately to the heart of my theme, then, what I propose is to imagine ourselves reasoning with a fellow mortal who is on such terms with life that the only comfort left him is to brood on the assurance "you may end it when you will." What reasons can we plead that may render such a brother (or sister) willing to take up the burden again? Ordinary Christians, reasoning with would-be suicides, have little to offer them beyond the usual negative "thou shalt not." God alone is master of life and death, they say, and it is a blasphemous act to anticipate his absolving hand. But can *we* find nothing richer or more positive than this, no reflections to urge whereby the suicide may actually see, and in all sad seriousness feel, that in spite of adverse appearances even for him life is worth living still? There are suicides and suicides – in the United States about three thousand of them every year – and I must frankly confess that with perhaps the majority of these my suggestions are impotent to deal. Where suicide is the result of insanity or sudden frenzied impulse, reflection is impotent to arrest its headway; and cases like these belong to the ultimate mystery of evil concerning which I can only offer considerations tending towards religious patience at the end of this hour. My task, let me say now, is practically narrow, and my words are to deal only with that metaphysical *tedium vitae* which is peculiar to reflecting men. Most of you are devoted for good or ill to the reflective life. Many of you are students of philosophy, and have already felt in your own persons the scepticism and unreality that too much grubbing in the abstract roots of things will breed. This is, indeed, one of the regular fruits of the over-studious career. Too much questioning and too little active responsibility lead, almost as often as too much sensualism does, to the edge of the slope, at the bottom of which lie pessimism and the nightmare or suicidal view of life. But to the diseases which reflection breeds, still further reflection can oppose effective remedies; and it is of the melancholy and *Weltschmerz* bred of reflection that I now proceed to speak.

Let me say immediately that my final appeal is to nothing more recondite than religious faith. So far as my argument is to be destructive, it will consist in nothing more than the sweeping away of certain views that often keep the springs of religious faith compressed; and so far as it is to be constructive it will consist in holding up to the light of day certain considerations calculated to let loose these springs in a normal, natural way. Pessimism is essentially a religious disease. In the form of it to which you are most liable it consists in nothing but a religious demand to which there comes no normal religious reply.

Now there are two stages of recovery from this disease, two different levels upon which one may emerge from the midnight view to the daylight view of things, and I must treat of them in turn. The second stage is the more complete and joyous, and it corresponds to the freer exercise of religious trust and fancy. There are, as is well known, persons who are naturally very free in this regard, others who are not at all so.

There are persons, for instance, whom we find indulging to their heart's content in prospects of immortality, and there are others who experience the greatest difficulty in making such a notion seem real to themselves at all. These latter persons are tied to their senses, restricted to their natural experience; and many of them moreover feel a sort of intellectual loyalty to what they call hard facts which is positively shocked by the easy excursions into the unseen that they witness other people make at the bare call of sentiment. Minds of either class may, however, be intensely religious. They may equally desire atonement, harmony, reconciliation, and crave acquiescence and communion with the total Soul of Things. But the craving, when the mind is pent in to the hard facts, especially as "Science" now reveals them, can breed pessimism, quite as easily as it breeds optimism when it inspires religious trust and fancy to wing their way to an other and a better world.

That is why I call pessimism an essentially religious disease. The nightmare view of life has plenty of organic sources, but its great reflective source in these days, and at all times, has been the contradiction between the phenomena of Nature and the craving of the heart to believe that behind Nature there is a spirit whose expression Nature is. What philosophers call natural theology has been one way of appeasing this craving. That poetry of nature in which our English literature is so rich has been another way. Now suppose a mind of the latter of our two classes, whose imagination is pent in consequently, and who takes its facts "hard"; suppose it, moreover, to feel strongly the craving for communion, and yet to realize how desperately difficult it is to construe the scientific order of Nature either theologically or poetically, and what result *can* there be but inner discord and contradiction? Now this inner discord (merely as discord) can be relieved in either of two ways. The longing to read the facts religiously may cease, and leave the bare facts by themselves. Or supplementary facts may be discovered or believed in, which permit the religious reading to go on. And these two ways of relief are the two stages of recovery, the two levels of escape from pessimism, to which I made allusion a moment ago, and which what follows will, I trust, make more clear.

III

Starting then with Nature, we naturally tend, if we have the religious craving, to say with Marcus Aurelius, O Universe, what thou wishest I wish. Our sacred books and traditions tell us of one God who made heaven and earth, and looking on them saw that they were good. Yet, on more intimate acquaintance, the visible surfaces of heaven and earth refuse to be brought by us into any intelligible unity at all. Every phenomenon that we would praise there exists cheek by jowl with some contrary phenomenon that cancels all its religious effect upon the mind. Beauty and hideousness, love and cruelty, life and death keep house together in indissoluble partnership; and there gradually steals over us, instead of the old warm notion of a man-loving Deity, that of an awful Power that neither hates nor loves, but rolls all things together meaninglessly to a common doom. This is an uncanny, a sinister, a nightmare view of life, and its peculiar *Unheimlichkeit* or poisonousness lies expressly in our holding two things together which cannot possibly agree – in our clinging on the one hand to the demand that there shall be a living spirit of the whole, and, on the other, to the belief that the course of nature must be such a spirit's adequate manifestation and expression. It is in the contradiction between the supposed being of a spirit that encompasses and owns us and with which we ought to have some communion, and the character of such a spirit as revealed by the visible world's course, that this particular death-in-life paradox and this melancholy-breeding puzzle reside. Carlyle expresses the result in that chapter of his immortal *Sartor Resartus* entitled *The Everlasting No*. "I lived," writes poor Teufelsdröckh, "in a continual indefinite pining fear; tremulous, pusillanimous, apprehensive of I knew not what: it seemed as if all things in the Heavens above and the Earth beneath would hurt me; as if the Heavens and the Earth were but boundless Jaws of a devouring Monster, wherein I, palpitating, lay waiting to be devoured."

This is the first stage of speculative melancholy. No brute can have this sort of melancholy, no man that is irreligious can become its prey. It is the sick shudder of the frustrated religious demand, and not the mere necessary outcome of animal experience. Teufelsdröckh himself could have made shift to face the general chaos and bedevilment of this world's experiences very well were he not the victim of an originally unlimited trust and affection towards them. If he might meet them piecemeal, with no suspicion of any Whole expressing itself in them, shunning the bitter parts and husbanding the sweet ones, as the occasion served, and as (to use a vulgar phrase) he struck it fat or lean, he could have zigzagged fairly towards an easy end, and felt no obligation to make the air vocal with his lamentations. The mood of levity, of "I don't care," is for this world's ills a sovereign and practical anaesthetic. But no! something deep down in Teufelsdröckh and in the rest of us tells us that there *is* a spirit in things to which we owe allegiance and for whose sake we must keep up the serious mood, and so the inner fever and discord also are kept up – for Nature taken on her visible surface reveals no such spirit, and beyond the facts of Nature we are at the present stage of our inquiry not supposing ourselves to look.

Now, I do not hesitate frankly and sincerely to confess to you that this real and genuine discord seems to me to carry with it the inevitable bankruptcy of natural religion naïvely and simply taken. There were times when Leibnitzes with their heads buried in monstrous wigs could compose Theodicies, and when stall-fed officials of an established church could prove by the valves in the heart and the round ligament of the hip joint the existence of a "Moral and Intelligent Contriver of the World." But those times are past; and we of the nineteenth century, with our evolutionary theories and our mechanical philosophies, already know nature too impartially and too well to worship unreservedly any god of whose character she can be an adequate expression. Truly all we know of good and beauty proceeds from nature, but none the less so all we know of evil. Visible nature is all plasticity and indifference, a moral multiverse, as one might call it, and not a moral universe. To such a harlot we owe no allegiance; with her as a whole we can establish no moral communion; and we are free in our dealings with her several parts to obey or destroy, and to follow no law but that of prudence in coming to terms with such of her particular features as will help us to our private ends. If there be a divine Spirit of the universe, Nature, such as we know her, cannot possibly be its *ultimate word* to man. Either there is no spirit revealed in nature, or else it is inadequately revealed there; and (as all the higher religions have assumed) what we call visible nature, or *this* world, must be but a veil and surface show whose full meaning resides in a supplementary unseen or *other* world.

I cannot help, therefore, accounting it on the whole a gain (though it may seem for certain poetic constitutions a very sad loss) that the naturalistic superstition, the worship of the god of nature simply taken as such should have begun to loosen its hold upon the educated mind. In fact, if I am to express my personal opinion unreservedly, I should say (in spite of its sounding blasphemous at first to certain ears) that the initial step towards getting into healthy ultimate relations with the universe is the act of rebellion against the idea that such a God exists. Such rebellion essentially is that which in the chapter quoted a while ago Carlyle goes on to describe:

Wherefore, like a coward, dost thou forever pip and whimper, and go cowering and trembling? Despicable biped! ... Hast thou not a heart; canst thou not suffer whatsoever it be; and, as a Child of Freedom, though outcast, trample Tophet itself under thy feet, while it consumes thee? Let it come, then; I will meet it and defy it!' And as I so thought, there rushed like a stream of fire over my whole soul; and I shook base Fear away from me forever. ...

Thus had the Everlasting No pealed authoritatively through all the recesses of my being, of my Me; *and then was it that my whole* Me *stood up, in native God-created majesty, and recorded its Protest. Such a Protest, the most important transaction in life, may that same Indignation and Defiance, in a psychological point of view, be fitly called. The Everlasting No had said: "Behold, thou art fatherless, outcast, and the Universe is mine"; to which my whole Me now made answer: "I am not thine, but Free, and forever hate thee!" "From that hour," Teufelsdröckh-Carlyle adds, "I began to be a man."*

And our poor friend, James Thomson, similarly writes:

Who is most wretched in this dolorous place?
I think myself; yet I would rather be
My miserable self than He, than He
Who formed such creatures to his own disgrace.

The vilest thing must be less vile than Thou
From whom it had its being, God and Lord!
Creator of all woe and sin! abhorred,
Malignant and implacable! I vow

That not for all Thy power furled and unfurled,
For all the temples to Thy glory built.
Would I assume the ignominious guilt
Of having made such men in such a world.

We are familiar enough in this community with the spectacle of persons exulting in their emancipation from belief in the God of their ancestral Calvinism, him who made the garden and the serpent and pre-appointed the eternal fires of hell. Some of them have found humaner Gods to worship, others are simply converts from all theology; but both alike they assure us that to have got rid of the sophistication of thinking they could feel any reverence or duty towards that impossible idol gave a tremendous happiness to their souls. Now, the idol of a worshipful spirit of Nature also leads to sophistication; and in souls that are religious and would also be scientific, the sophistication breeds a philosophical melancholy from which the first natural step of escape is the denial of the idol; and with the downfall of the idol, whatever lack of positive joyousness may remain, there comes also the downfall of the whimpering and cowering mood. With evil simply taken as such, men can make short work, for their relations with it then are only practical. It looms up no longer so spectrally, it loses all its haunting and perplexing significance as soon as the mind attacks the instances of it singly and ceases to worry about their derivation from the "one and only Power".

Here, then, on this stage of mere emancipation from monistic superstition, the would-be suicide may already get encouraging answers to his question about the worth of life. There are in most men instinctive springs of vitality that respond healthily when the burden of metaphysical and infinite responsibility rolls off. The certainty that you now *may* step out of life whenever you please, and that to do so is not blasphemous or monstrous, is itself an immense relief. The thought of suicide is now no longer a guilty challenge and obsession.

This little life is all we must endure.
The grave's most holy peace is ever sure.

says Thomson; adding, "I ponder these thoughts, and they comfort me." Meanwhile we can always stand it for twenty-four hours longer, if only to see what tomorrow's newspaper will contain or what the next postman will bring. But far deeper forces than this mere vital curiosity are arousable, even in the pessimistically-tending mind; for where the loving and admiring impulses are dead, the hating and fighting impulses will still respond to fit appeals. This evil which we feel so deeply is something which we can also help to overthrow, for its sources, now that no "Substance" or "Spirit" is behind them, are finite, and we can deal with each of them in turn. It is, indeed, a remarkable fact that sufferings and hardships do not, as a rule, abate the love of life; they seem, on the contrary, usually to give it a keener zest. The sovereign source of melancholy is repletion. Need and struggle are what excite and inspire us; our hour of triumph is what brings the void. Not the Jews of the captivity, but those of the days of Solomon's glory are those from whom the pessimistic utterances in our Bibles come. Germany, when she lay trampled beneath the hooves of Bonaparte's troopers, produced perhaps the most optimistic and idealistic literature that the world has seen; and not till the French "milliards" were distributed after 1871 did pessimism overrun the country in the shape in which we see it there today. The history of our own race is one long commentary on the cheerfulness that comes with fighting ills. Or take the Waldenses, of whom I lately have been reading, as examples of what strong men will endure.

In 1485, a papal bull of Innocent VIII enjoined their extermination. It absolved those who should take up the cross against them from all ecclesiastical pains and penalties, released them from any oath, legitimized their title to all property which they might have illegally acquired, and promised remission of sins to all who should kill the heretics.

"There is no town in Piedmont," says a Vaudois writer, "where some of our brethren have not been put to death. Jordan Terbano was burnt alive at Susa; Hippolite Rossiero at Turin; Michael Goneto, an octogenarian, at Sarcena; Vilermin Ambrosio hanged on the Col di Meano; Hugo Chiambs, of Fenestrelle, had his entrails torn from his living body at Turin; Peter Geymarali of Bobbio in like manner had his entrails taken out in Luzerne, and a fierce cat thrust in their place to torture him further; Maria Romano was buried alive at Rocca Patia; Magdalena Fauno underwent the same fate at San Giovanni; Susanna Michelini was bound hand and foot and left to perish of cold and hunger on the snow at Sarcena ; Bartolomeo Fache, gashed with sabres, had the wounds filled up with quicklime, and perished thus in agony at Fenile; Daniel Michelini had his tongue torn out at Bobbo for having praised God; James Baridari perished covered with sulphurous matches which had been forced into his flesh under the nails, between the fingers, in the nostrils, in the lips, and all over the body and then lighted; Daniel Rovelli had his mouth filled with gunpowder which, being lighted, blew his head to pieces; (...) Sara Rostignol was slit open from the legs to the bosom,

and left so to perish on the road between Eyral and Luzerna; Anna Charbonnier was impaled, and carried thus on a pike from San Giovanni to La Torre." *

Und dergleichen mehr! In 1630, the plague swept away one-half of the Vaudois population, including fifteen of their seventeen pastors. The places of these were supplied from Geneva and Dauphiny, and the whole Vaudois people learned French in order to follow their services. More than once their number fell by unremitting persecution from the normal standard of twenty-five thousand to about four thousand. In 1686, the Duke of Savoy ordered the three thousand that remained to give up their faith or leave the country. Refusing, they fought the French and Piedmontese armies till only eighty of their fighting men remained alive or uncaptured, when they gave up and were sent in a body to Switzerland.

But in 1689, encouraged by William of Orange and led by one of their pastor-captains, between eight hundred and nine hundred of them returned to capture their old homes again. They fought their way to Bobi, reduced to four hundred men in the first half year, and met every force sent against them until

---

* *Quoted by George E. Waring in his book on Tyrol.*

at last the Duke of Savoy, giving up his alliance with that abomination of desolation, Louis XIV, restored them to comparative freedom. Since which time they have increased and multiplied in their barren Alpine valleys to this day.

What are our woes and sufferance compared with these? Does not the recital of such a fight so obstinately waged against such odds fill us with resolution against *our* petty powers of darkness, machine politicians, spoilsmen, and the rest? Life is worth living, no matter what it bring, if only such combats may be carried to successful terminations and one's heel set on the tyrant's throat. To the suicide, then, in his supposed world of multifarious and immoral Nature, you can appeal, and appeal in the name of the very evils that make his heart sick there, to wait and see *his* part of the battle out. And the consent to live on, which you ask of him under these circumstances, is not the sophistical "resignation" which devotees of cowering religions preach. It is not resignation in the sense of licking a despotic deity's hand. It is, on the contrary, a resignation based on manliness and pride. So long as your would-be suicide leaves an evil of *his own* unremedied, so long he has strictly *no concern* with evil in the abstract and at large. The submission which you demand of yourself to the general fact of evil in the world, your apparent acquiescence in it, is here nothing but the conviction that evil at large is *none of your business* until your business with your private particular evils is liquidated and settled up. A challenge of this sort, with proper designation of detail, is one that need only be made to be accepted by men whose normal instincts are not decayed, and your reflective would-be suicide may easily be moved by it to face life with a certain interest again. The sentiment of honour is a very penetrating thing. When you and I, for instance, realize how many innocent beasts have had to suffer in cattle-cars and slaughter-pens and lay down their lives that we might grow up, all fattened and clad, to sit together here in comfort and carry on this discourse, it does, indeed, put our relation to the Universe in a more solemn light. "Does not," as a young Amherst philosopher (Xenos Clark, now dead) once wrote, "the acceptance of a happy life upon such terms involve a point of honour?" Are we not bound to do some self-denying service with our lives in return for all those lives upon which ours are built? To hear this question is to answer it in only one possible way, if one have a normally constituted heart!

Thus, then, we see that mere instinctive curiosity, pugnacity, and honour may make life on a purely naturalistic basis seem worth living from day to day to men who have cast away all metaphysics in order to get rid of hypochondria, but who are resolved to owe nothing as yet to religion and its more positive gifts. A poor halfway stage, some of you may be inclined to say; but at least you must grant it to be an honest stage; and no man should dare to speak meanly of these instincts which are our nature's best equipment, and to which religion herself must in the last resort address her own peculiar appeals.

notion that this physical world of wind and water, where the sun rises and the moon sets, is absolutely and ultimately the divinely aimed at and established thing, is one that we find only in very early religions, such as that of the most primitive Jews. It is this natural religion (primitive still in spite of the fact that poets and men of science whose goodwill exceeds their perspicacity keep publishing it in new editions tuned to our contemporary ears) that, as I said a while ago, has suffered definitive bankruptcy in the opinion of a circle of persons, amongst whom I must count myself, and who are growing more numerous every day. For such persons the physical order of nature, taken simply as Science knows it, cannot be held to reveal any one harmonious spiritual intent. It is mere *weather*, as Chauncey Wright called it, doing and undoing without end. Now I wish to make you feel, if I can in the short remainder of this hour, that we have a right to believe that the physical order is only a partial order; we have a right to supplement it by an unseen spiritual order which we assume on trust, if only thereby life may seem to us better worth living again. But as such a trust will seem to some of you sadly mystical and execrably unscientific, I must first say a word or two to weaken the veto which you may consider that Science opposes to our act. There

IV

And now, in turning to what religion may have to say to the question, I come to what is the soul of my discourse. Religion has meant many things in human history, but when from now onward I use the word I mean to use it in the supernaturalist sense, as declaring that the so-called order of nature that constitutes this world's experience is only one portion of the total Universe, and that there stretches beyond this visible world an unseen world of which we now know nothing positive, but in its relation to which the true significance of our present mundane life consists. A man's religious faith (whatever more special items of doctrine it may involve) means for me essentially his faith in the existence of an unseen order of some kind in which the riddles of the natural order may be found explained. In the more developed religions this world has always been regarded as the mere scaffolding or vestibule of a truer, more eternal world, and affirmed to be a sphere of education, trial, or redemption. One must in some fashion die to this world before one can enter into life eternal. The is included in human nature an ingrained naturalism and materialism of mind which can only admit facts that are actually tangible. Of this sort of mind the entity called "Science" is the idol. Fondness for the word "scientist" is one of the notes by which you may know its votaries; and its short way of killing any opinion that it disbelieves in is to call it "unscientific." It must be granted that there is no slight excuse for this. Science has made such glorious leaps in the last three hundred years, and extended our knowledge of Nature so enormously both in general and in detail; men of science, moreover, have as a class displayed such admirable virtues, that it is no wonder if the worshippers of Science lose their head. In this very University, accordingly, I have heard more than one teacher say that all the fundamental conceptions of truth have already been found by Science, and that the future has only the details of the picture to fill in. But the slightest reflection on the real conditions will suffice to show how barbaric such notions are. They show such a lack of scientific imagination, that it is hard to see how one who is actively advancing any part of Science can make a mistake so crude. Think how many absolutely new scientific conceptions have arisen in our own generation, how many new problems have been formulated that were never thought of before, and then cast an eye upon the brevity of Science's career. It began with Galileo just three hundred years ago. Four thinkers since Galileo, each informing his successor of what discoveries his own lifetime had seen achieved, might have passed the torch of Science into our hands as we sit here in this room. Indeed, for the matter of that, an audience much smaller than the present one, an audience of some five or six score people, if each person in it could speak for his own generation, would carry us away to the black unknown of the human species, to days without a document or monument to tell their tale. Is it credible that such a mushroom knowledge, such a growth overnight as this, *can* represent more than the minutest glimpse of what the Universe will really prove to be when adequately understood? No! our Science is a drop, our ignorance a sea. Whatever else be certain, this at least is certain: that the world of our present natural knowledge *is* enveloped in a larger world of *some* sort of whose residual properties we at present can frame no positive idea.

Agnostic positivism, of course, admits this principle theoretically in the most cordial terms, but insists that we must not turn it to any practical use. We have no right, this doctrine tells us, to dream dreams, or *suppose* anything about the unseen part of the universe, merely because to do so may be for what we are pleased to call our highest interests. We must always wait for sensible evidence for our beliefs; and where such evidence is inaccessible we must frame no hypotheses whatever. Of course this is a safe enough position *in abstracto*. If a thinker had no stake in the unknown, no vital needs, to live or languish according to what the unseen world contained, a philosophic neutrality and refusal to believe either one way or the other would be his wisest cue. But, unfortunately, neutrality is not only inwardly difficult, it is also outwardly unrealizable, where our relations to an alternative are practical and vital. This is because, as the psychologists tell us, belief and doubt are living attitudes, and involve conduct on our part. Our only way, for example, of doubting, or refusing to believe, that a certain thing *is*, is continuing to act as if it were *not*. If, for instance, we refuse to believe that the room is getting cold, we must leave the windows open and light no fire just as if it still were warm. If I refuse to believe that you are worthy of my confidence, I must keep you uninformed of all my secrets just as if you were *un*worthy of the same. And similarly if, as the agnostics tell me, I must not believe that the world *is* divine, I can only express that refusal by declining ever to act distinctively as if it were so, which can only mean acting on certain critical occasions as if it were *not* so, or in an unmoral and irreligious way. There are, you see, inevitable occasions in life when inaction is a kind of action and must count as action, and when not to be *for* is to be practically *against*. And in all such cases strict and consistent neutrality is an unattainable thing.

And after all, isn't this duty of neutrality where only our inner interests would lead us to believe, the most ridiculous of commands? Isn't it sheer dogmatic folly to say that our inner interests *can* have no real connection with the forces that the hidden world *may* contain? In other cases divinations based on inner interests have proved prophetic enough. Take Science herself! Without an imperious inner demand on our part for ideal, logical, and mathematical harmonies, we should never have attained to proving that such harmonies lie hidden between all the chinks and interstices of the crude natural world. Hardly a law has been established in Science, hardly a fact ascertained, that was not first sought after, often with sweat and blood, to gratify an inner need. Whence such needs come from we do not know – we find them in us, and biological psychology so far only classes them with Darwin's "accidental variations." But the inner need of believing that this world of nature is a sign of something more spiritual and eternal than itself is just as strong and authoritative in those who feel it, as the inner need of uniform laws of causation ever can be in a professionally scientific head. The toil of many generations has proved the latter need prophetic. Why may not the former one be prophetic, too? And if needs of ours outrun the visible universe, why may not that be a sign that an invisible universe is there? What, in short, has authority to *debar* us from trusting our religious demands? Science as such assuredly has no authority, for she can only say what is, not what is not; and the agnostic "thou shalt not believe without coercive sensible evidence" is simply an expression (free to any one to make) of private personal appetite for evidence of a certain peculiar kind.

Now, when I speak of trusting our religious demands, just what do I mean by "trusting"? Is the word to carry with it license to define in detail an invisible world and to anathematize and excommunicate those whose trust is different? Certainly not! Our faculties of belief were not primarily given us to make orthodoxies and heresies withal; they were given us to live by. And to trust our religious demands means first of all to live in the light of them, and to act as if the invisible world which they suggest were real. It is a fact of human nature that men can live and die by the help of a sort of faith that goes without a single dogma or definition. The bare assurance that this natural order is not ultimate but a mere sign or vision, the external staging of a many-storied universe, in which spiritual forces have the last word and are eternal; this bare assurance is to such men enough to make life seem worth living in spite of every contrary presumption suggested by its circumstances on the natural plane. Destroy this inner assurance, vague as it is, however, and all the light and radiance of existence is extinguished for these persons at a stroke. Often enough the wild-eyed look at life – the suicidal mood will then set in.

And now the application comes directly home to you and me. Probably to almost every one of us here the most adverse life would seem well worth living, if we only could be *certain* that our bravery and patience with it were terminating and eventuating and bearing fruit somewhere in an unseen spiritual world. But granting we are not certain, does it then follow that a bare trust in such a world is a fool's paradise and lubberland, or rather that it is a living attitude in which we are free to indulge ? Well, we are free to trust at our own risks anything that is not impossible and that can bring analogies to bear in its behalf. That the world of physics is probably not absolute, all the converging multitude of arguments that make in favour of idealism tend to prove. And that our whole physical life may lie soaking in a spiritual atmosphere, a dimension of Being that we at present have no organ for apprehending, is vividly suggested to us by the analogy of the life of our domestic animals. Our dogs, for example, are *in* our human life but not *of* it. They witness hourly the outward body of events whose inner meaning cannot, by any possible operation, be revealed to their intelligence, events in which they themselves often play the cardinal part. My terrier bites a teasing boy, for example, and the father demands damages. The dog may be present at every step of the negotiations, and see the money paid without an inkling of what it all means, without a suspicion that it has anything to do with *him*. And he never *can* know in his natural dog's life. Or take another case which used greatly to impress me in my medical-student days. Consider a poor dog whom they are vivisecting in a laboratory. He lies strapped on a board and shrieking at his executioners, and to his own dark consciousness is literally in a sort of hell. He cannot see a single redeeming ray in the whole business; and yet all these diabolical-seeming events are usually controlled by human intentions with which, if his poor benighted mind could only be made to catch a glimpse of them, all that is heroic in him would religiously acquiesce. Healing truth, relief to future sufferings of beast and man are to be bought by them. It is genuinely a process of redemption. Lying on his back on the board there he is performing a function incalculably higher than any prosperous canine life admits of; and yet, of the whole performance, this function is the one portion that must remain absolutely beyond his ken.

Now turn from this to the life of man. In the dog's life we see the world invisible to him because we live in both worlds. In human life, although we only *see* our world, and his within it, yet encompassing both these worlds a still wider world may be there as unseen by us as our world is by him; and to believe in that world *may* be the most essential function that our lives in this world have to perform. But "*may* be! *may* be!" one now hears the positivist contemptuously exclaim; "what use can a scientific life have for maybes?" Well, I reply, the "scientific" life itself has much to do with maybes, and human life at large has everything to do with them. So far as man stands for anything, and is productive or originative at all, his entire vital function may be said to be to deal with maybes. Not a victory is gained, not a deed of faithfulness or courage is done, except upon a maybe; not a service, not a sally of generosity, not a scientific exploration or experiment or textbook, that *may* not be a mistake. It is only by risking our persons from one hour to another that we live at all. And often enough our faith beforehand in an uncertified result *is the only thing that makes the result come true*. Suppose, for instance, that you are climbing a mountain and have worked yourself into a position from which the only escape is by a terrible leap. Have faith that you *can* successfully make it, and your feet are nerved to its accomplishment. But mistrust yourself, and think of all the sweet things you have heard the scientists say of *maybes*, and you will hesitate so long that, at last, all unstrung and trembling, and launching yourself in a moment of despair, you roll in the abyss. In such a case (and it belongs to an enormous class), the part of wisdom as well as of courage is to *believe what is in the line of your needs*, for only by the belief is the need fulfilled. Refuse to believe, and you shall indeed be right, for you shall irretrievably perish. But believe, and again you shall be right, for you shall save yourself. You *make* one or the other of two possible universes true by your trust or mistrust, both universes having been only *maybes* in this particular, before you contributed your act.

Now, it appears to me that the question whether life is worth living is subject to conditions logically much like these. It does, indeed, depend on you the liver. If you surrender to the nightmare view and crown the evil edifice by your own suicide, you have indeed made a picture totally black. Pessimism, completed by your act, is true beyond a doubt, so far as your world goes. Your mistrust of life has removed whatever worth your own enduring existence might have given to it; and now, throughout the whole sphere of possible influence of that existence, the mistrust has proved itself to have had divining power. But suppose, on the other hand, that instead of giving way to the nightmare view you cling to it that this world is not the *ultimatum*. Suppose you find yourself a very well-spring, as Wordsworth says, of

Zeal, and the virtue to exist by faith
As soldiers live by courage; as, by strength
Of heart, the sailor fights with roaring seas.

Suppose, however thickly evils crowd upon you, that your unconquerable subjectivity proves to be their match, and that you find a more wonderful joy than any passive pleasure can bring in trusting ever in the larger whole. Have you not now *made* life worth living on *these* terms? What sort of a thing would life really be, with *your* qualities ready for a tussle with it, if it only brought fair weather and gave these higher faculties of yours no scope? Please remember that optimism and pessimism are definitions of the world, and that our own reactions on the world, small as they are in bulk, are integral parts of the whole thing, and necessarily help to determine the definition. They may even be the decisive elements in determining the definition. A large mass can have its unstable equilibrium overturned by the addition of a feather's weight. A long phrase may have its sense reversed by the addition of the three letters *n, o, t*. This life *is* worth living, we can say, s*ince it is what we make it, from the moral point of view*, and we are determined to make it from that point of view, so far as we have anything to do with it, a success. Now, in this description of faiths that verify themselves I have assumed that our faith in an invisible order is what inspires those efforts and that patience of ours that make this visible order good for moral men. Our faith in the seen world's goodness (goodness now meaning fitness for successful moral and religious life) has verified itself by leaning on our faith in the unseen world. But will our faith in the unseen world similarly verify itself? Who knows? Once more it is a case of *maybe*. And once more *maybes* are the essence of the situation. I confess that I do not see why the very existence of an invisible world *may* not in part depend on the personal response which any one of us may make to the religious appeal. God himself, in short, *may* draw vital strength and increase of very being from our fidelity. For my own part, I do not know what the sweat and blood and tragedy of this life mean, if they mean anything short of this. If this life be not a real fight, in which something is eternally gained for the Universe by success, it is no better than a game of private theatricals from which one may withdraw at will. But it *feels* like a real fight; as if there were something really wild in the Universe which we, with all our idealities and faithfulnesses, are needed to redeem. And first of all to redeem our own hearts from atheisms and fears. For such a half-wild, half-saved universe our nature is adapted. The deepest thing in our nature in this *Binnenleben* (as a German doctor lately has called it), this dumb region of the heart in which we dwell alone with our willingnesses and unwillingnesses, our faiths and fears. As through the cracks and crannies of subterranean caverns the earth's bosom exudes its waters, which then form the fountainheads of springs, so in these crepuscular depths of personality the sources of all our outer deeds and decisions take their rise. Here is our deepest organ of communication with the nature of things; and compared with these concrete movements of our soul all abstract statements and scientific arguments, the veto, for example, which the strict positivist pronounces upon our faith, sound to us like mere chatterings of the teeth. For here possibilities, not finished facts, are the realities with which we have actively to deal; and to quote my friend William Salter, of the Philadelphia Ethical Society, "as the essence of courage is to stake one's life on a possibility, so the essence of faith is to believe that the possibility exists."

These, then, are my last words to you: Be not afraid of life. Believe that life *is* worth living, and your belief will help create the fact. The "scientific proof" that you are right may not be clear before the day of judgment (or some stage of Being which that expression may serve to symbolize) is reached. But the faithful fighters of this hour, or the beings that then and there will represent them, may then turn to the fainthearted, who here decline to go on, with words like those with which Henry IV greeted the tardy Crillon after a great victory had been gained: "Hang yourself, brave Crillon! we fought at Arques, and you were not there."

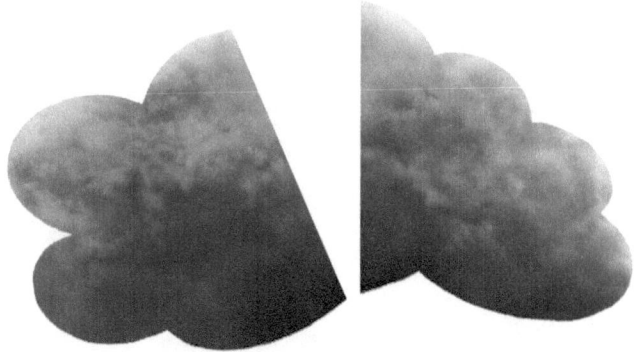

www.ingramcontent.com/pod-product-compliance
Lightning Source LLC
Chambersburg PA
CBHW020331010526
44107CB00054B/2066